Under Dark Waters: Surviving the *Titanic*

*To Pat*

*With best wishes
and may your ship
never sink!*

*Anna*

*AWP 2019
Portland.*

# *under* DARK WATERS

## SURVIVING THE *TITANIC*

POEMS BY
Anna M. Evans

*Anna*

ABLE MUSE PRESS

# Able Muse Press

www.ablemusepress.com

Printed in the United States of America

Library of Congress Control Number: 2018931566

ISBN 978-1-77349-012-0 (paperback)
ISBN 978-1-77349-013-7 (digital)

Cover image: "Survivor Surfaces" by Alexander Pepple

Cover & book design by Alexander Pepple

Able Muse Press is an imprint of *Able Muse:* A Review of Poetry, Prose & Art—at
www.ablemuse.com

Able Muse Press
467 Saratoga Avenue #602
San Jose, CA 95129

April is the cruelest month . . .

—T. S. Eliot

# *Acknowledgments*

I am grateful to the editors of the following journals where many of these poems originally appeared, sometimes in earlier versions:

*Peacock Journal:* "Casualties of Fast Living"
"Paradelle for the Wreck"
"Under Class"
"Sister Ships"
"Curse of the *Titanic*, I"

*Mezzo Cammin:* "Animals of the *Titanic*"
"On Visiting the *Titanic* Exhibition in Vegas
with My Teenage Daughters"
"A Wreath for Rosie Gray"

*Measure:* "A Tune to Remember"

Thank you to the Virginia Center for Creative Arts, where most of these poems were written during a two-week residency.

*Foreword*

THIS IS A SMALL BOOK that packs a very large punch, and then another equally large punch, and then another. It takes on a very large emotion-fraught subject, then it takes on a second equally large emotion-fraught subject, then it weaves the two together so that each becomes an analogy to, and commentary on, its counterpart. To belabor the metaphor a bit, the final knock-out punch is the extraordinary panoply of skill and technical dexterity with which the whole intricate conglomerate of emotion and subject matter is presented to us.

It's difficult to talk about the book and not risk spoiling some of the startling effects that are in store for any first-time reader of it, so I must necessarily be a little sketchy about what is to come. The book opens with a sequence of poems on the sinking of the *Titanic*. Like the fateful voyage itself, we begin with celebration and lists of wonders; then we are given hints of what is to come, including a lovely vignette of a woman traveling on the ship who is reading a novel about the wreck of the largest passenger ship yet built, called *The Titan*, published fourteen years before the *Titanic*'s maiden voyage (this novel really exists). The anecdote almost sounds like one of Hardy's *Life's Little Ironies*, and sure enough a homage to Hardy's "Convergence of the Twain" is waiting for us further in the sequence. Because we know what is to happen, the hints resonate ever more grimly, until we are in the midst of the disaster itself.

Then, and I hope this is not giving too much away, we have an extraordinary transition poem called "A Meditation on Loss" which begins by commenting on the difficulty of mentally grasping the immensity of a disaster like the *Titanic*'s sinking and the subsequent largely needless loss of life, and ends, startlingly enough:

> These deaths don't move me more than any other,
> but every day I live, I miss my mother.

This is a huge risk, as we have heard nothing about the poet's mother previous to this moment, and in isolation, in the way it can seem almost uninterestedly dismissive of the book's subject matter to this point, it can only read as perilously close to bathos. But the poem introduces the second major subject of the book, which is the journey the poet's mother took in her last illness, and the circumstances of her death. Once we read these poems, and then go back and reread the *Titanic* poems, we see how the book's first half is not there only for itself, which it triumphantly is, but as a preparation for the much more searing and intimate personal loss described in the second half. And the second half not only gives us the story of the poet's mother's death, but also interweaves it with the reality of the disastrous voyage that is the first half's subject, so that the transition is not merely a turning to a new subject but a deepened elaboration of the first half's themes, which themselves become a public historical analogy to private grief experienced in the present. Structural complexity like this is not easy to bring off, and it is a remarkable tribute to the poet's skill that she manages these dual focuses so deftly and substantially, so that they complement and comment on each other rather than get in one another's way.

This is skill on the macro level, but the skill evident in these poems on the micro level should also be noted. Many of the poems are sonnets, and the whole sequence ends with a crown of sonnets, an almost impossibly tricky technical feat. Besides sonnets there are a number of forms that repeat lines (a villanelle, a rondeau, a paradelle,) or phrases (a beautifully turned ghazal), and there is an eighteen-line poem in monorhyme, and as if that weren't enough there is also a pastiche blues and a dexterous parody of the whole of Auden's "In Memory of W. B. Yeats."

But despite the great accomplishment of these technical tours de force, it is not admiration for technique that is the main feeling that stays with a reader once the book is finished; rather it is the undeniably powerful emotional force of what is being said. Perhaps paradoxically, there can be no higher praise for technique than this—that it becomes incidental for us as we register and respond to what the poems are saying, since it is precisely through technique that the saying is happening, and in its happening moving us.


—Dick Davis

# Contents

*vi*   Acknowledgments

*vii*   Foreword

I

*5*   Sister Ships

*6*   Attempting the First Six-Day Crossing

*7*   *Titanic* Bill of Lading (Partial)

*8*   Futility, or the Wreck of the *Titan*

*9*   Distress Signals

*11*   And the Band Was Playing Ragtime

*12*   *Titanic* Blues

*13*   A Tune to Remember

*14*   Chief Baker Charles Joughin and His Whisky

*15*   Three Captains' Tales

*18*   Under Class

*20*   The Lord's Prayer on Collapsible B

*22*   Animals of the *Titanic*

*23*   Life Cycle of the Iceberg

*24*   Sinking a Few

*25*   The Confidence Man

*26*   The Unsinkable Molly Brown

*27*   "God Himself Could Not Sink This Ship"

*29*   Paradelle for the Wreck

30   In Memory of the *Titanic*

34   Curse of the *Titanic*, I

35   Curse of the *Titanic*, II – Madeleine Astor

36   A Meditation on Loss

## II

39   Entering the Ice Field

40   On Watching James Cameron's *Titanic* While Pregnant
     with My Second Child

41   On Visiting the *Titanic* Exhibition in Vegas with My
     Teenage Daughters

42   My Father and I, and Our Wine

43   I Made Mistakes yet More Could Have Been Done

45   Casualties of Fast Living

46   Ghosts

47   *Titanic* Month

## III

51   A Wreath for Rosie Gray

Under Dark Waters: Surviving the *Titanic*

I

It seems to me that the disaster about to occur was the event that not only made the world rub its eyes and awake but woke it with a start keeping it moving at a rapidly accelerating pace ever since with less and less peace, satisfaction, and happiness. To my mind the world of today awoke April 15th, 1912.

— Jack B. Thayer, *Titanic* Survivor

# Sister Ships

What an experience—traveling on the *Olympic!*
She is the flagship of the White Star line.
Compared to other ships she looks gigantic—
the epitome of luxury in design.
Her first class cabins are spacious and opulent.
She has a Turkish bath, a swimming pool;
many passengers are prominent
in high society. She is a jewel!
This is a truly marvelous time to be rich.
(It isn't quite so comfy in third class)
and if by chance the voyage hits a glitch,
an iceberg, say, nothing will come to pass.
She is unsinkable. No need to fear.
Look at her, waiting at Southampton pier.

Look at her, waiting at Southampton pier.
She is unsinkable. No need to fear
an iceberg, say. Nothing will come to pass,
even if the voyage should hit a glitch.
(It may not be so comfy in third class).
This is a truly marvelous time to be rich
in high society. She is a jewel.
Many passengers are prominent.
She has a Turkish bath, a swimming pool.
Her first class cabins are spacious and opulent—
the epitome of luxury in design.
Compared to other ships she is gigantic—
the perfect flagship of the White Star line.
What an experience, traveling on the *Titanic!*

# Attempting the First Six-Day Crossing

> Captain E.J. Smith ignored or discounted a total
> of seven iceberg warnings from other ships and his
> own crew.
>
> —*History of the* Titanic

Under the stars this cloudless night,
the sea lies smooth as a marble tomb
that the ship cuts cleanly, all decks bright
under the stars. This cloudless night
the iceberg looms like a work of spite
by a god, contemptuous when men presume.
Under the stars this cloudless night,
the sea lies, smooth as a marble tomb.

# *Titanic* Bill of Lading (Partial)

A Found Poem

Wakem & McLaughlin, 42 case wines

Spaulding & Brothers, 34 case athletic goods

Maltus & Ware, 8 case orchids

Isler & Guve, 4 bales straw

Rawstick Trading Company, 28 bags sticks

Dujardin & Ladnick, 10 box melons

Tiffany & Company, 1 cask china

American Express Company, 1 case Edison gramophones, 1 case
speedometers

Strohmeyer & Arpe, 75 bales fish

Wright & Graham Company, 437 casks tea

Brown Brothers & Company, 76 case dragon's blood, 100 case
shelled walnuts

Stechert, G.E. & Company, 12 package periodicals

Vandegrift, F.B. & Company, 63 case champagne

Downing, R.F. & Company, 1 case iron jacks

Sanger, R. & Company, 3 case hair nets

Pape, Chas. & Company, 1,196 bags potatoes

Simon, A.I. & Company, 1 case raw feathers

Broadway Trust Company, 3 case coney skins (rabbit)

Acker, Merrall & Condit, 75 case anchovies, 225 case mussels

Bernard, Judas & Company, 70 bundles cheese

Knauth, Nachod & Kuhne, 107 case mushrooms

On order: 4 case opium, 2 case grandfather clocks, 12 case
ostrich feathers

# Futility, or the Wreck of the *Titan*

> The *Titan* and its sinking have been noted to be
> very similar to the real-life passenger ship RMS
> *Titanic,* which sank fourteen years later.
>
> —*Wikipedia*

The first-class ladies have their reading room.
We have the library—that's where I repair
after dinner. (My husband, I assume
is smoking with the other men.) The chair
I like is snug and in a well-lit nook.
I finished *Ethan Frome* the other night.
Today I found the most unsettling book
by Morgan Robertson—it tells the plight
of an ocean liner just like the *Titanic*
except it hits an iceberg and then sinks!
Imagine how the passengers all panic.
I had to ask my husband what he thinks.
He said I shouldn't worry my pretty head—
it's only fiction. No one's really dead.

# Distress Signals

The *Titanic* was not the first ship to send an SOS
despite what the legend says. Still we believe
there is a certain glamor in distress.
First Radio Officer Phillips sent CQD times five.

Despite what the legend says, we believe
the *Californian* could have saved more lives.
First Radio Officer Phillips sent CQD times five
but there was no one left awake to receive.

The *Californian* could have saved some lives
if she hadn't been at a dead stop, beset by ice
with no one left awake to receive
when Second Radio Officer Bride added the SOS.

Both ships lay at a dead stop, beset by ice,
the *Titanic* holed and sinking, sending up flares,
when Second Radio Officer Bride added the SOS
with the *Carpathia* already answering his prayers.

The *Titanic,* holed and sinking, sent up eight flares,
tapped out Morse code: "CQD, SOS."
The *Carpathia* was already answering her prayers
while the nearer ship did nothing at all because

the Morse codes tapped out, "CQD, SOS,"
weren't acronyms, just coded signals for help.
The nearer ship did nothing at all because
the men who could have understood were asleep.

Not acronyms, just coded signals for help.
The disaster meant the rules changed forever
because the men who should have understood were asleep.
Humans learn from failure because we're clever.

The disaster meant the rules changed forever.
After the *Titanic* it was *Save Our Souls, SOS*—
humans learn from failure because we're clever
and there is a certain glamor in distress.

# And the Band Was Playing Ragtime

Bandmaster Wallace Henry Hartley had assembled
his men, and the band was playing ragtime.
— Walter Lord, *A Night to Remember*

"Women and children first!" the purser cries.
The deck's tilt can no longer be ignored.
Seeing the rigid faces, the wild eyes,
Hartley gathers his boys, and strikes a chord.
Sweet syncopation rises in the air,
jaunty rhythms that soothe the frightened crowd.
*Look,* sings his violin, *this is how men dare*
*make tunes that break the rules, and play them loud.*

The engines are silent now, so the music sways
doomed men in steerage who grin and tap their feet,
brave men who share a smoke as the octet plays
melodies pulsing with life in every beat—
all know the cold, hard death they're about to face.
In the end, courage is all about the bass.

# *Titanic* Blues

James Cameron's blockbuster didn't include any
mention of Joseph Laroche, a Haitian-born, French-
educated engineer traveling with his family who is
believed to have been the only black man among
the passengers on the *Titanic*.

—*Chicago Tribune*

I couldn't get a decent job in France
No, they don't like men as dark as me in France
I thought in Haiti we might have a chance

The ship we booked on wasn't for my family
Nothing means more to me than my family
They didn't want my children in their nursery

So I switched our tickets to the White Star Line
I'd heard good things about the White Star Line
That new *Titanic* ship appeared so fine

I thought then things were looking up for me
Yes, things were surely looking up for me
We were traveling home in luxury

I woke my family when the iceberg hit
My kids were scared because the iceberg hit
I got them to a boat, told them to sit

I knew there wouldn't be a place for me
I thought I'd have a place in history
But there's no place for men as dark as me.

# A Tune to Remember

The Legend is, of course, that the band went down
playing "Nearer My God to Thee."
— Walter Lord, *A Night to Remember*

Now that the boats have been lowered to the sea,
now that the lights have failed, and a deeper chill
sets in among those remaining, the melody
starts to sound frivolous in a night so still,
so full of portent. Song sheets lit by stars,
Hartley flips through, finds nothing with the power
to be the last song, the one listed in memoirs
by the exclusive survivors of this hour.

And so he plays—by instinct or by ear—
something that sounds a little like a hymn
that he doesn't quite recall. The bandsmen hear
and by some miracle they all join in,
a tune never played before or heard again—
that unique night's unnamable refrain.

# Chief Baker Charles Joughin and His Whisky

> Maynard held out his hand and Joughin hung on, treading
> water, still thoroughly insulated.
>> — Walter Lord, *A Night to Remember*

I'd counted boats and knew there weren't enough.
It seemed a fair assumption I would die.
Well, I'm from Liverpool and pretty tough—
no hero, just an ordinary guy.
I helped them load the boats till they were full,
threw deck chairs off for floating just in case
and every now and then I took a pull
of whisky I had hidden in my space.

So when *Titanic* dropped I felt no pain.
They say the water was a little cold,
no worse than slogging through the Mersey rain,
my veins on fire with all that liquid gold.
For hours I paddled in the demon drink,
watched sober swimmers give up hope and sink.

# Three Captains' Tales

I

SS *Californian* – Mistakes Were Made

> Had assistance been promptly proffered, or had the
> wireless operator of the *Californian* remained a few
> minutes longer at his post, that ship might have had
> the proud distinction of rescuing the lives of the
> passengers and crew of the *Titanic*.
>
> —US Senate Subcommittee Report

Disasters need someone to take the blame.
The night *Titanic* sank I was in bed
but found it hard to sleep, and so I read
until the officer of the Night Watch came
and told me he'd seen rockets. I still claim
my duty first was to the men I led,
not to those people drowning, soon to be dead.
I couldn't have saved them all, and feel no shame.

My tiny ship, not even fifty crew,
two lifeboats. Had I crawled through our own ice
and reached the swimmers, pulled a few aboard,
they would have swamped us. *Titanic*'s lifeboats, too,
were slow to return, aware there'd be a price.
Compassion's a weakness a captain can't afford.

II

RMS *Carpathia* – If Only I Could Have Done More

> On receiving the first SOS from *Titanic* at 12.15,
> Cottam raised Captain Rostron who had already
> retired for the night, and Rostron in turn rose to
> the challenge of his first maritime emergency with
> impeccable practical thoroughness.
>
> — "*Carpathia*'s Role in *Titanic*'s Rescue"

Thank God the wireless man was late to bed.
Alas, I struggled to believe his claim—
which countered every single word I'd read
on the *Titanic*. When confirmation came
I roused all hands to work. The stokers led
my charge to raise our speed, and zero blame
should rest upon them for so many dead.
That count remains my own one lifelong shame.

Five minutes, ten? But once I woke my crew
each man worked harder than he could afford
to ready the ship—and certain passengers too—
then bring survivors straggling aboard.
Yet though we steamed at top speed through the ice
I saw the bodies, pay each night the price.

III

RMS *Titanic* – A Captain Goes Down

> It is believed that Ismay may have influenced
> Captain Smith to ignore the ice warnings and steam
> ahead at full speed.
>
> —*Titanicstory.com*

I shouldn't have listened to Ismay—*It's just ice,*
*and we're unsinkable*—an absurd claim!
The White Star Line could charge a higher price
for a six-day crossing, true. And yet the blame
is mine. I should have vetoed him. The crew
and all the people comfortable in bed
relied on me. I've failed *Titanic* too.
I followed when I know I should have led.

How beautiful she was, that day I came
upon her in dry dock, black, white and red—
a jewel that I've ruined, to my shame,
along with all of those who'll end up dead.
To pay the penalty I must afford,
I grip the tilting rail, last man on board.

# Under Class

Mary refused to be parted from John under the
women and children first edict and [was] lost in the
sinking.
　　—*Encyclopedia Titanica*

Black ice in my veins.
I can't see my husband John,
the man I stayed with.

Sleep pulls me under.
I can't see John, my husband.
Someone's crying out.

Sleep pulls me under,
beneath the water again.
Someone's crying out.

*In the name of God.*
Beneath the water again,
my mouth full of brine.

In the name of God,
can anybody hear us?
My mouth full of brine.

Freezing bitter tears.
Can anybody hear us?
The boats are far off.

Freezing bitter tears
cannot summon them near us.
The boats so far off.

The man I stayed with
cannot summon them near us.
Black ice in my veins.

# The Lord's Prayer on Collapsible B

Someone said, "Don't you think we ought to pray?"
and so we went around and each man named
the religion that he followed here on earth.
I'm a Presbyterian, like my father
but I'd have prayed to any God to deliver
us right then, and after, sought forgiveness.

When facing death, men need to feel forgiven,
and even the ungodly turn to prayer.
On the upturned boat we had scant hope of delivery.
I thought of my wife and children, whispered their names.
And then we agreed we should all say the "Our Father"
and hope for a better place beyond this earth.

My God, I yearned to be back on solid earth
more than I wanted my many sins forgiven.
I wanted to hear my young son call out, "Father!"
and gather my family together in simple prayer.
Still, one man there—I do not know his name—
took a deep breath and commenced at once to deliver

the Lord's Prayer, the one that prays for Him to deliver
us from evil, that His will be done on earth.
I almost laughed! To think this happened in his name!
Some sinner perhaps on the ship, he couldn't forgive?
Anyway, I mumbled the well-known prayer.
All of us, shivering, repeated the "Our Father."

A young boy whimpered that he had lost his father.
The screams of the drowning faded beyond deliverance,
and still a dozen or more of us said the prayer
known since childhood to so many people on earth.
"Forgive us," I said to the dying. "Please forgive
me as I forgive you," and mentioned people by name.

Finally a whistle, and a dark shape asking to name
who was in charge. I said the name of my father
uneasily, aware that there could be no forgiveness
even if by some miracle we were delivered.
I knew I'd spend the rest of my days on earth
thinking of those who did not have a prayer.

Nor would I ever name my most honest prayer:
"Our Father, for our hubris on this earth,
forgive your children, and O Lord, deliver us."

# Animals of the *Titanic*

Astor's Airedale, Kitty, perished along with her owner
Ben, Captain Smith's Irish Wolfhound, put ashore in Southampton
Chow Chow, left behind by Harry Anderson, drowned
Dog, a Fox Terrier, last seen swimming
English Foxhounds, one hundred, booked on alternate passage
Frou Frou, detached from her grip on Helen Bishop's gown, perished
Gamin de Pycombe, prizewinning French Bulldog, drowned
Hens and roosters, caged, drowned
Isham, Ann Elizabeth and her Great Dane, bodies recovered together
Jenny, ship's mouser, drowned
Kittens of Jenny, likewise
Lady, Pomeranian of First Class passenger Margaret Hays, survived
Mice and rats, free-living, drowned
Newfoundland Rigel, survivor and hero, apocryphal
Objections raised to the three dogs on the lifeboats, none
Pomeranian belonging to Elizabeth Rothschild, survived
Quote: "I refuse to get on the lifeboat without my dog."
Rothschild, Martin, body never recovered
Sun Yat Sen, Pekinese of Henry Sleeper Harper, survived
Terrier and Spaniel of the Philadelphia Carters, perished
Unconscionable, the fifty-six children left out of the lifeboats
Vacancies on the lifeboats, forty percent
Wealthy survivors, two hundred plus three dogs
And XYZ, and XYZ, and XYZ

# Life Cycle of the Iceberg

> The ideal murder weapon is probably an icicle, because you
> can melt the evidence once you've committed the crime.
> —Simon Brett

Atoms are constant, but when they take a form
it has a finite life. Though icebergs are old
they leave no evidence when it gets warm.

Three thousand years ago or more, a storm
set down a layer of snow in which, we're told,
atoms were constant in their solid form.

As more snow fell, pressure worked to transform
to ice the snow the icecap could not hold,
and left no evidence. When it got warm

the ice squeezed out through cracks, which is the norm—
the way that glaciers have always rolled
out, atoms constant in a solid form.

The glacier's end is weak, nonuniform,
and slabs detach, like snapping from a mold,
then leave. No evidence, when it gets warm

remains of the iceberg that did so much harm.
Only the sea, its spots of awful cold—
the atoms constant, not in solid form,
the evidence all gone when it gets warm.

# Sinking a Few

> Coffey deserted the *Titanic* at Queenstown. . . .
> Reports stated that he had had a foreboding of
> disaster, possibly a fire.
>
> —*Encyclopedia Titanica*

I always tell the story in the pub—
it's a sure way to keep myself in beer,
like being part of an exclusive club.
Explaining how I woke that day in fear,
my dream a swirl of smoke and shouting men
and how I couldn't shift the sense of dread,
makes people fill my tankard up again—
the thrill of listening to the almost dead.

The truth I hide is somewhat less exciting—
there was this girl I knew in Queenstown city.
She had another beau, we fell to fighting
for which of us would go home with the Pretty.
She left with someone else. We both stayed drunk
for days. Next thing I know, *Titanic*'s sunk.

# The Confidence Man

If saved, inform my sister, Mrs. J. F. Adams of
Findlay, Ohio. Lost. [Signed] J. H. Rogers.

    —Note handed to woman in lifeboat

It's instinct. Sometimes even I don't know
what makes me stick, or draw, or double down.
I was winning when I felt the glancing blow,
but something told me not to hang around.
Then, when I reached A deck and heard the plan
was women and children first, I kept my cool.
Two years of living as a wanted man
had taught me how to circumvent a rule.

Still, faking my own death was quite the play!
That woman's face as she took and read my note
was priceless, then I quietly slipped away,
and wrapped in a shawl, got on another boat.
So, thank God for our mishap with the ice.
Here comes New York, a con man's paradise.

# The Unsinkable Molly Brown

The myth of "Molly" Brown has very little to do with
the real life of Margaret Tobin Brown, although it
speaks to her spirit.

—*Encyclopedia Titanica*

I don't suppose you know she ran for senate,
eight years before a woman could even vote?
That she worked for human rights? That's why each tenet
she lived by told her to turn back the boat.
I doubt you know what she did in the Great War,
or care how many languages she spoke.
The minute that she seized the lifeboat's oar,
her life began to dwindle to a joke.

Please know that no one ever called her Molly.
She was respected everywhere she went
until that movie. Reynolds, pert and jolly,
portrayed her without the family's consent.
Amusing maybe, but the plot was junk—
that's how the truth of Margaret got sunk.

# "God Himself Could Not Sink This Ship"

Dim moon-eyed fishes near
    Gaze at the gilded gear
And query: "What does this vaingloriousness down here?" ...
    — Thomas Hardy, "The Convergence of the Twain"


The largest ship in the world she was,
with even a swimming pool,
nine hundred feet from bow to stern,
nine decks from bridge to keel,
with new triple-screw propeller blades
that were a bitch to steer,
a grand staircase of carved red oak
in William and Mary style.
Yet now, to her crystal chandelier
dim moon-eyed fishes near.

Fleet said, "Iceberg, dead ahead!"
and Hitchens yanked the wheel.
Then the huge berg struck the sluggish ship,
grazing the starboard hull.
In first class, high above the breach,
the impact was unclear.
But below, the sea came pouring in
and the forward bulkheads fell.
And now the sharks that all men fear
gaze at the gilded gear.

The Astors and the Rothschilds, roused
from luxury, stayed cool,
the women in the lifeboats,
the men, top hats and tails.
She took three hours to list and fill
and finally disappear.
All fifty thousand tons of her
and fifteen hundred souls.
Now spider crabs come by to peer
and query: "What does this vaingloriousness down here?"

# Paradelle for the Wreck

For seventy years the wreck's undisturbed bed.
For seventy years the wreck's undisturbed bed.
Spider crabs and brittle starfish the only passengers.
Spider crabs and brittle starfish the only passengers.
The undisturbed wreck's only passengers—spider crabs
and starfish—for seventy years the brittle bed.

Man always seeks to find what has been lost.
Man always seeks to find what has been lost.
In the end, the image of a boiler on the sandy floor.
In the end, the image of a boiler on the sandy floor.
Man always seeks the image of what has been lost—
to find in the end a boiler on the sandy floor.

Since then, salvage missions, official and clandestine.
Since then, salvage missions, official and clandestine.
All submarine bumps leave a mark on the hull.
All submarine bumps leave a mark on the hull.
Salvage missions since then all leave a mark,
and on the official hull, clandestine submarine bumps.

For seventy years a boiler bumps spider crabs
and only starfish leave a mark on the undisturbed bed.
Since then, submarine missions, official and clandestine,
find the image of passengers on the sandy floor.
Man seeks to salvage all. In the end,
the wreck's always what has been lost—the brittle hull.

# In Memory of the *Titanic*

After W. H. Auden

I

She disappeared in a wintry clime.
The seas were frozen, the promenades almost deserted,
and although there was no snow
the lookouts shivered in the crow's nest
with no instruments save their eyes.
The day of her death was a cold, dark day.

Far from her destruction,
New York and London bustled with bankers,
the soon-to-be widowed slept in their beds.
By vague telegrams,
the death of the great ship was kept from the stockbrokers.

But for her it was her last evening as herself,
an evening of bridge and merriment.
Then the bulkheads failed her.
The minds of her engineers grew blank.
Seawater invaded the mail room.
The thrum of her engines stopped. She became her legend.

Now she is scattered among a hundred stories
and wholly given over to Hollywood
to find her happiness in immortality

or be dismissed under a modern code of conscience.
The tales of a dead ship
are modified in the imagination of the living.


But in the importance and noise of the twenty-first century
when the politicians are lying like traitors on the Senate floor
and the poor still have their sufferings to which they are fairly
　　accustomed
and each in the light of his smartphone is almost convinced of his
　　freedom,
a few thousand will think of this day
as one thinks of a day when one did something slightly unusual.


No instruments save the lookouts' eyes.
The day of her death was a cold, dark day.

## II

You were the icon of a golden era—
catering, no, pandering, to the rich,
an epoch poised on the brink of the muddy ditch
Europe would soon become in a bloody war.
Poetry makes nothing happen, but it can remind
us *how* things happen, that man is dull and blind
to risks when measured against his avarice.
You were the glorious Queen of the world, designed
to rule the seas. You thought they would be kind
but they were full of ice.

## III

Seas, receive an honored guest.
The *Titanic*'s laid to rest.
Let the Anglo-Irish ship
to the ocean bottom slip.

Let the brokers count the cost
for the goods and lives we lost.
But they were not lost in vain.
It will never happen again.

Many changes will be made
in the wake of the charade
of the lack of boats and sense.
They will spare no sound expense.

Though you rot on the seabed
with your crew of silent dead,
yet the stories will pile high
and your name will never die.

# Curse of the *Titanic,* I

Tragic ship *Titanic* was cursed, the press claimed.
Headline story: "Mummy of Amen-Ra sinks!"
Lurid tales of ghosts and Egyptian horrors
easy to swallow.

Supernatural terrors are like excuses—
not the fault of anyone human, blameless
Captain Smith and Ismay, unlucky victims
brought down by evil.

Lies, all lies. No mummy aboard *Titanic*
walked the deck or steered at the iceberg's flank. But
stupid men who thought they could beat the odds is
harder to live with.

# Curse of the *Titanic,* II – Madeleine Astor

She carried her doubts with her always, like her pearls.
    —Enzo Fiermonte

After the wreck she thinks, what could be worse?
Eighteen, widowed, a baby on the way,
and though John Jacob left her a pretty purse,
if she remarries, the trust will cease to pay.

She sticks it for four years, but then wants more.
After the wreck, she thinks, what could be worse?
But husband two is something of a bore,
so seeking escape from her narrow universe

she meets a man en voyage, the complete inverse
of all she knows, a common Italian boxer.
After the wreck she thinks, what could be worse?
*He* is, of course—he bullies her and knocks her.

And when she leaves, he sells her to *True Story*.
A laughing stock, she takes an overdose—
PTSD, perhaps, or allegory.
After the wreck she thought, what could be worse?

# A Meditation on Loss

Oh, they built the ship *Titanic,* to sail the ocean blue.
For they thought it was a ship that water would never go through.
It was on its maiden trip, that an iceberg hit the ship.
It was sad when the great ship went down.
  —Children's Song


When death arrives on such a monstrous scale
it feels unreal, which is, of course, made worse
by all the ways that we retell the tale—
in stories, movies, songs, and even verse.
Add to this how strange that world can sound
with its rigid social structure and quaint clothes—
a moral fable, fifteen hundred drowned
through arrogance. The fact is no one knows
quite how we measure loss. It's not by lives—
thousands die daily—diseases, famine, war.
Is it the grief of the person who survives
that makes a single loss hard to ignore?
These deaths don't move me more than any other,
but every day I live, I miss my mother.

II

And it wasn't until we were in the lifeboat and rowing away, it wasn't until then I realized that ship's going to sink. It hits me there.

— Eva Hart, *Titanic* Survivor

# Entering the Ice Field

Each year, on my father's birthday, I called home
and my mother answered. Then, one year, she didn't.
My father said she couldn't come to the phone.
It was a lie, or at best, a semi-truth.
I gave him his greetings, asked to speak to her.
He said she couldn't, that she was in the bath.
So I offered to call back later, but I knew
the way birds scatter before an impending storm
something was waiting for us, impossibly big,
looming, unavoidably in our path.
Somewhen, somewhere, in a different future
he takes the phone to her as he always did,
and we chatter mindlessly, her head in a towel—
I can hear the water sloshing around—
until she says she needs to dry her hair.
That day, I continued, on high alert,
knowing something was wrong, and still we forged
full speed ahead as though the seas were clear
when all along the ice was waiting for us.

# On Watching James Cameron's *Titanic*
## While Pregnant with My Second Child

I cried an ocean the night I saw
that film I'd never watched before
because my eldest was twelve weeks old
back when the picture first hit gold.
Now, I was six months gone once more.

Rose, shivering on the wooden door,
Celine's voice haunting the movie score,
Jack, teeth chattering at the cold,
my daughter kicking in my hold,
I cried an ocean.

*It's only hormones,* I wept and swore,
my mothering heart exposed and raw.
In my head I knew I was being sold
the lamest fantasy ever told.
Yet, aware what I was sobbing for,
I cried an ocean.

# On Visiting the *Titanic* Exhibition in Vegas with My Teenage Daughters

> I'm the King of the World!
>> —Jack Dawson, James Cameron's *Titanic*

*Trust me,* I say, *you're going to be enthralled.*
Curious, they wander toward the model ship.
They are the undisputed Queens of the world.

The bills of lading, the lists of people killed,
aren't that exciting to them. I bite my lip.
*Trust me,* I'd said, *you're going to be enthralled.*

But then we enter a room that's kept so cold
the genuine iceberg loses barely a drip.
They are the undisputed Queens of the world.

And next a chamber where a swathe of the hold
brought from the seabed is set up, a vertical strip.
*Trust me,* I'd said. I think they are enthralled.

Of course, there's a place where the movie set's installed
from the famous scene. *This won't be cheap,* I quip,
but they are the undisputed Queens of the world.

My youngest stands at the bow, her arms unfurled.
Her sister steadies her, one hand upon her hip.
*Trust me,* she says. I can only watch, enthralled.
They are the undisputed Queens of the world.

# My Father and I, and Our Wine

It took four weeks, my mother's slow decline—
he had his coping methods, I had mine,
and then the one we both shared, which was wine.
I'd drive back from the hospital and dine
on food he had prepared—the meals were fine,
I think, but might as well have reeked of brine
for all the notice I spared to consign
to them. More critically, I would incline
my silver goblet his way—shimmer shine
in the candlelight, while steadily the line
on the Merlot dropped like a sinking ship, a sign
that things we didn't speak of or define
evaded our control. Without design
he'd open another bottle—how benign
the ruby liquid, blood of a far off vine,
numbing my nerves while strengthening my spine
for the new tomorrow I needed to resign
myself to face, bone-chilling and malign.

# I Made Mistakes yet More Could Have Been Done

I made mistakes, yet more could have been done.
They should have seen that she was very ill.
The antibiotic wasn't the strongest one.
I couldn't save her through my force of will.

It's been a year—I wake up crying still.
If only I'd insisted that we run
to emergency, instead of waiting till
I made mistakes. Yet more could have been done—

her doctors knew she'd fought cancer and won,
but now got sick from just a little chill.
When they sent her home with drugs, like anyone,
they should have seen that she was very ill.

I watched her try to swallow every pill.
She spat up phlegm as soon as she'd begun
to eat. In hospital she went downhill.
The antibiotic wasn't the strongest one.

I thought she was breathing food, and told someone.
The nurses fetched the doctor, who said, "Nil
by mouth." They upped and upped the oxygen.
I couldn't cure her through my force of will.

They put the tube in and my voice got shrill.
She breathed as if her rib cage weighed a ton,
sedated . . . a coma. At last I chose to kill
the machines. A couple of hours, and it was done.
I made mistakes.

# Casualties of Fast Living

A sudden fluttering motion drew my eye
toward the windshield wiper on the right—
a large and richly patterned butterfly
was pinioned there, wings split, and wedged in tight.
And I was doing seventy on a road
with no hard shoulder, couldn't stop for five
long miles. I pulled to the inside lane, and slowed,
knew from her flailing legs she was alive.

At last a pebbled strip appeared. I braked,
gingerly lifted the arm, assessed her plight.
Her abdomen was crushed. My spirit ached.
I prized her off and she attempted flight,
but failed. I moved her to a grassy bed,
said prayers for all of those I've left for dead.

# Ghosts

We all have our ghosts. For you the worst month
is July. Sunshine, fireworks. Your nephew jumped off a bridge.
How can you stand the celebrations when you're down?

*Titanic* lies on the sea bed, twelve-thousand feet down,
found in 1985 on the first day of the ninth month.
Divers have now swum through the bridge

and the smoking room where the men played bridge.
Don't ask what your nephew thought on the way down.
We resign ourselves to the ghosts of the month.

Every month *Titanic*'s bridge sinks further down.

# *Titanic* Month

I flew three thousand miles to be by her side in April
but found out there was nowhere I could hide in April.

I thought to make things right by force of will,
to celebrate her fifty-one years a bride in April.

I hugged her, read to her, fed her, even changed her.
Please understand, God knows I really tried in April.

Nurses scurried about, the machines beeped
alarmingly, and still the doctors lied in April.

Each night I left the hospital the stars
were witnesses to all the tears I cried in April.

No deals to make, no good choices, no prayers.
No wonder then, that I was terrified in April.

*Titanic* month, as pitiless as ice
to all the souls she's drowned. My mother died in April.

# III

The sounds of people drowning are something that I can not describe to you, and neither can anyone else. It's the most dreadful sound and there is a terrible silence that follows it.

— Eva Hart, *Titanic* Survivor

# A Wreath for Rosie Gray

I

There is a moment right before disaster
when everything is perfect. I can see
*Titanic* forging through the ice field, faster
than any ship before her. Then there's me,
observing the date, about to call my father.
We're so wrapped up in things, we hardly know
with lives this trouble-free, we ought to rather
pause them if we could, or take them slow.

But time continues its relentless pace,
events unfold in fixed and linear motion.
Never again, that smile upon my face
before I dial their number. There's an ocean
of grief before us, not quite yet in sight.
The well-lit ship speeds onward in the night.

## II

The well-lit ship speeds onward in the night;
the lookout sees the iceberg, calls it in.
The ship evades it. Everything's all right!
With hindsight, there are many ways to win.
Yet, at the time perhaps you see the danger
but cannot grasp exactly what it means.
In real life, conditions are much stranger
than anything in glossy magazines.

In fifteen years abroad, I'd never not
connected with my mother on the phone.
My father sounded vague, a bit distraught,
and could I call back later? So we postpone
full knowledge of our issues and their bulk,
the looming iceberg's black and massive hulk.

## III

The looming iceberg's black and massive hulk
materializes, frighteningly near.
Alarms sound, but *Titanic*'s powerful bulk
is slow to turn. The bridge is fraught with fear.
I call my parents back, this time insist
on speaking to my mother. She's all wrong—
unlike herself. I wonder if I'd missed
some signs that this was happening all along.

I prize out facts: a cough, a new prescription,
now this confusion no one understands.
It's hard to gauge the threat from the description,
but they could use another pair of hands.
So I assess my duty as a daughter,
consider crossing miles of open water.

IV

Consider crossing miles of open water—
the ship *Titanic* decked out like no other.
The triple expansion engines that had brought her
this far shut off. Now silence reigns.
                                    My mother
meanwhile garbles nonsense. Somehow I
will set my life at anchor, leave it frozen,
make my Atlantic passage. Of course, I'll fly.
It's not, perhaps, the spring break I'd have chosen.

But I must see what's happening. The only way
is go and look. I'm hoping there's an answer—
a different drug? Someone prepared to say
the doctor's wrong? Remind them she beat cancer?
I make the trip alone and ill at ease.
Sometimes we find ourselves in unknown seas.

## V

Sometimes we find ourselves in unknown seas.
To call a ship unsinkable tempts fate,
to *act* like that naively is to tease
such fate beyond endurance. Still we create
these myths—what child can see her parents dying?
We build in safety features to prevent
catastrophes; there must be things worth trying.
*Titanic*'s bulkheads make their steep descent.

The breached compartments hiss as they are sealed.
The bridge is warm and noisy with relief.
Though there are those on board who know this shield
won't hold, for now they foster the belief
that *Titanic* will not sink. Like them I fight
the fear that everything is not all right.

VI

The fear that everything is not all right
moves like gossip through the stirring ship.
Clearly the lowest decks aren't watertight,
whatever was said about her maiden trip.
The truth is that she's making water fast.
We change my mother's pills. Her cough gets worse,
the things she says and does that must be classed
as odd have multiplied. We call the nurse.

A bladder infection's breezily suggested.
Apparently this turns old people funny.
We send a urine sample to get tested,
but the NHS is stretched and short of money
and no one says the name of a disease.
It's just like dying slowly, by degrees.

# VII

It's just like dying slowly by degrees.
Captain Smith conducts a full inspection,
concludes *Titanic*'s had it, and agrees
it's time to lower the boats.
                              There's no infection
in my mother's urine. We change her pills again
and watch her constantly. She eats odd things,
pours her expensive perfume down the drain,
pretends to text on card tables, and sings.

That night she vomits, pees herself and strips.
I carry her to the bathroom like a child,
pull her panties up round skinny hips.
Next day she's unrecognizable, and wild,
lashes out blindly, falls into a sulk.
These are the nightmares where our demons skulk.

VIII

These are the nightmares where our demons skulk—
*Titanic*'s tilting hard toward the bow
because the water's overflowed the bulk-
heads. All the passengers have woken now.
We follow my mother to the hospital—
she isn't getting better, we can't cope.
I get home late. Exhaustion takes its toll.
I fall asleep, and in my dream, there's hope.

Hope springs eternal . . . etc. Next day I find
she's had pneumonia all along. I think
that maybe they can cure her now? Her mind
seems clearer.
                    There's little doubt the ship will sink.
Tipped forward, listing starboard in the water.
The brave keep busy, do not think of slaughter.

## IX

The brave keep busy, do not think of slaughter.
I teach my college course by remote control,
visit my mum twice daily, the good daughter,
fix the little things and avoid the whole,
sit at home each night with my dad and drink.
Women and children first, goes out the call.
Everyone knows *Titanic*'s going to sink
while I grade papers, trying not to bawl.

How could they launch the ship with so few boats?
They move my mother to intensive care.
Still the iron inside me somehow floats
even as she's drowning in the air,
even as my side is pierced by fear.
The SOS gets sent but no one's near.

X

The SOS gets sent but no one's near.
I call my brother in Australia
but he can't come—the wrong time of the year.
Toward *Titanic,* the *Carpathia*
is steaming at a reckless rate of knots.
My mother fights for every single breath—
they want to intubate her, ask for my thoughts.
They will not say it, but the risk is death.

The risk of *life* is death, I think, and worse,
there are no odds of evading it at all.
I call my brother again, am brutal, terse.
He still can't come. I weep as I end the call.
*Do it,* I tell the doctors, suddenly brave.
If luck holds out there may be life to save.

## XI

If luck holds out there may be life to save.
Sedated, her oxygen levels are on the rise.
*Titanic* snaps and drops to her watery grave,
the freezing sea alive with the swimmers' cries.
How peaceful it must be, where she settles under
the numbing currents, muffling the noise above.
I read my mother poetry and wonder
if she can hear me, if she feels my love.

Many are dead in fifteen minutes or less,
not by drowning, but from the lethal cold.
My mother's fingers turn blue. I repossess
her wedding ring, a simple band of gold.
Like ghosts the staff appear and disappear
in random waves. There are no constants here.

## XII

In random waves there are no constants. Here
comes the new doctor now. Her brain scan's back.
I grip my father's hand, and swallow a tear,
try to follow: three strokes, a heart attack.
No hope of full recovery.
                    One boat
rowed back to the wreck to pick up people dying.
The rest, too scared they wouldn't stay afloat,
shivered till silence dispossessed the crying.

How do you let another die, and live?
They said it was our choice, turn off the machines
or not.
           How can the ones who live forgive
themselves and carry on their same routines?
I sent my father home. It wasn't brave.
*Is* the first place of death the actual grave?

XIII

Is the first place of death the actual grave?
It was for many souls who died that day,
their bodies lost. Still, *Carpathia* did save
some seven hundred and five, gone on their way
to New York City.
                          I leave my mother's side
both numb and raw. A friend will drive me home.
She opened her eyes just once before she died,
and looked past me, her gaze as bright as chrome.

I search for something tender and profound,
but death is neither—it's pointless and it's cheap
and needn't have happened.
                          Fifteen hundred drowned
or frozen to death, their futures lost in the deep.
Listen to them: Trust in no God, they warn.
We are all orphans as soon as we are born.

## XIV

We are all orphans as soon as we are born.
Mother, I miss you. A tiny tragedy.
No movie version to heap with praise or scorn.
My dad and your son will soon be visiting me—
yes, I forgave him. All of us make our choices.
Every day on earth is like a gamble.
This poem's a way of gathering human voices
against the dark, and mainly in preamble.

Life's a short trip with just one destination,
then there's a nothing deeper than the sea.
Some people die alone, some in congregation,
some I don't care about, some mean the world to me.
Most of the time I'm glad that I was born.
There is nothing to do but live and mourn.

## XV

The well-lit ship speeds onward. In the night,
the looming iceberg's black and massive hulk.
These are the nightmares where our demons skulk.
The fear that everything is not all right—
it's just like dying slowly, by degrees.
Consider crossing miles of open water—
sometimes we find ourselves in unknown seas.
The brave keep busy, do not think of slaughter.

The SOS gets sent but no one's near.
If luck holds out there may be life to save.
In random waves there are no constants. Here
is the first place of death, the actual grave.
We are all orphans as soon as we are born.
There is nothing to do but live and mourn.

ANNA M. EVANS' POEMS HAVE appeared in the *Harvard Review, Atlanta Review, Rattle, American Arts Quarterly,* and *32 Poems.* She gained her MFA from Bennington College, and is the editor of the *Raintown Review.* Recipient of Fellowships from the MacDowell Artists' Colony and the Virginia Center for the Creative Arts, and winner of the 2012 Rattle Poetry Prize Readers' Choice Award, she  currently teaches at West Windsor Art Center and Rowan College at Burlington County.

*Under Dark Waters: Surviving the Titanic* was the runner-up for the 2017 Able Muse Book Award.

# Also from Able Muse Press

Jacob M. Appel, *The Cynic in Extremis – Poems*

William Baer, *Times Square and Other Stories;*
*New Jersey Noir – A Novel*

Lee Harlin Bahan, *A Year of Mourning (Petrarch) – Translation*

Melissa Balmain, *Walking in on People (Able Muse Book Award for Poetry)*

Ben Berman, *Strange Borderlands – Poems;*
*Figuring in the Figure – Poems*

Lorna Knowles Blake, *Green Hill (Able Muse Book Award for Poetry)*

Michael Cantor, *Life in the Second Circle – Poems*

Catherine Chandler, *Lines of Flight – Poems*

William Conelly, *Uncontested Grounds – Poems*

Maryann Corbett, *Credo for the Checkout Line in Winter – Poems;*
*Street View – Poems*

John Philip Drury, *Sea Level Rising – Poems*

Rhina P. Espaillat, *And after All – Poems*

D. R. Goodman, *Greed: A Confession – Poems*

Margaret Ann Griffiths, *Grasshopper – The Poetry of M A Griffiths*

Katie Hartsock, *Bed of Impatiens – Poems*

Elise Hempel, *Second Rain – Poems*

Jan D. Hodge, *Taking Shape – carmina figurata;*
*The Bard & Scheherazade Keep Company – Poems*

Ellen Kaufman, *House Music – Poems*

Carol Light, *Heaven from Steam – Poems*

Kate Light, *Character Shoes – Poems*

April Lindner, *This Bed Our Bodies Shaped – Poems*

Martin McGovern, *Bad Fame – Poems*

Jeredith Merrin, *Cup – Poems*

Richard Moore, *Selected Poems;*
*Selected Essays*

Richard Newman, *All the Wasted Beauty of the World* – *Poems*

Alfred Nicol, *Animal Psalms* – *Poems*

Frank Osen, *Virtue, Big as Sin* (*Able Muse Book Award for Poetry*)

Alexander Pepple (Editor), *Able Muse Anthology;*
*Able Muse – a review of poetry, prose & art*
(semiannual, winter 2010 on)

James Pollock, *Sailing to Babylon* – *Poems*

Aaron Poochigian, *The Cosmic Purr* – *Poems;*
*Manhattanite* (*Able Muse Book Award for Poetry*)

Jennifer Reeser, *Indigenous* – *Poems*

John Ridland, *Sir Gawain and the Green Knight* (*Anonymous*) – *Translation*
*Pearl* (*Anonymous*) – *Translation*

Stephen Scaer, *Pumpkin Chucking* – *Poems*

Hollis Seamon, *Corporeality* – *Stories*

Ed Shacklee, *The Blind Loon: A Bestiary*

Carrie Shipers, *Cause for Concern* (*Able Muse Book Award for Poetry*)

Matthew Buckley Smith, *Dirge for an Imaginary World*
(*Able Muse Book Award for Poetry*)

Barbara Ellen Sorensen, *Compositions of the Dead Playing Flutes* – *Poems*

Rosemerry Wahtola Trommer, *Naked for Tea* – *Poems*

Wendy Videlock, *Slingshots and Love Plums* – *Poems;*
*The Dark Gnu and Other Poems;*
*Nevertheless* – *Poems*

Richard Wakefield, *A Vertical Mile* – *Poems*

Gail White, *Asperity Street* – *Poems*

Chelsea Woodard, *Vellum* – *Poems*

www.ablemusepress.com

CPSIA information can be obtained
at www.ICGtesting.com
Printed in the USA
FSHW01n2133010618
48733FS